W9-BHL-150

WITHDRAWN

THE HAMMERHEAD SHARK

By Sara Green

BELLWETHER MEDIA · MINNEAPOLIS, MN

Jump into the cockpit and take flight with Pilot books. Your journey will take you on high-energy adventures as you learn about all that is wild, weird, fascinating, and fun!

This edition first published in 2013 by Bellwether Media, Inc.

No part of this publication may be reproduced in whole or in part without written permission of the publisher. For information regarding permission, write to Bellwether Media, Inc., Attention: Permissions Department, 5357 Penn Avenue South, Minneapolis, MN 55419.

Library of Congress Cataloging-in-Publication Data

Green, Sara, 1964-
The hammerhead shark / by Sara Green.
    pages cm. – (Pilot. Shark fact files)
Audience: 8-12.
Summary: "Engaging images accompany information about the hammerhead shark. The combination of high-interest subject matter and narrative text is intended for students in grades 3 through 7"–Provided by publisher.
Includes bibliographical references and index.
ISBN 978-1-60014-871-2 (hardcover : alk. paper)
1. Hammerhead sharks–Juvenile literature. I. Title.
QL638.95.S7G74 2013
597.3'4–dc23

                          2012034021

TABLE OF CONTENTS

HAMMERHEAD SHARK
IDENTIFIED

Two divers descend into the deep blue waters off the coast of Cocos Island, Costa Rica. They hope to witness a spectacular sight. As they peer up at the sunlit waters above them, their wish comes true. A school of hammerhead sharks passes overhead. Each has a wide, flat head. The divers try to count them, but they soon give up. There are at least a hundred sharks. All too soon, the last of the sharks swim by on their way to deeper waters.

TELL-TALE HEAD

The scientific name for the hammerhead shark is *Sphyrna*, the Greek word for "hammer."

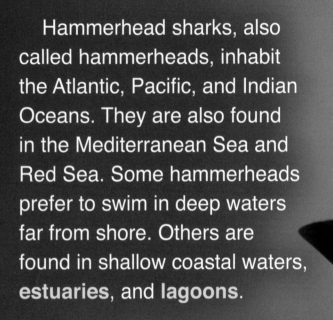

Hammerhead sharks, also called hammerheads, inhabit the Atlantic, Pacific, and Indian Oceans. They are also found in the Mediterranean Sea and Red Sea. Some hammerheads prefer to swim in deep waters far from shore. Others are found in shallow coastal waters, **estuaries**, and **lagoons**.

N
W **E**
S

☐ = **hammerhead shark territory**

Hammerheads often travel in schools during the day. At night the schools break up and the sharks hunt alone. Many hammerheads **migrate** together each year. They often prefer to swim off northern coastlines during spring and summer. When temperatures cool in the fall and winter, they travel south to warmer waters. Migrating schools can include hundreds of hammerheads.

There are nine **species** of hammerheads. All of them are known for their wide, flat heads called **cephalofoils**. Some cephalofoils are shaped like hammers, while others are shaped like shovels. These strange head shapes probably help the sharks make quick turns and move gracefully through water.

great hammerhead

HAMMERHEAD SPECIES

Bonnethead or Shovelhead
Great Hammerhead
Scalloped Bonnethead
Scalloped Hammerhead
Scoophead
Smalleye Hammerhead
Smooth Hammerhead
Whitefin Hammerhead
Winghead

scalloped
bonnethead

great hammerhead

human

The longest and heaviest type of hammerhead shark is
the great hammerhead. It can grow to be almost 20 feet
(6.1 meters) long and weigh up to 1,000 pounds
(454 kilograms). The scalloped bonnethead is the smallest
species. It measures around 3 feet (1 meter) long.

dorsal fins

Hammerheads have gray-brown backs and white bellies. This color pattern is an example of **countershading**. It allows hammerheads to blend in with the colors of the ocean and sneak up on prey.

A hammerhead's skeleton is made of **cartilage**. This lightweight tissue helps it bend and turn with ease. Its body is covered with scales called **dermal denticles**. These protect the shark from injury and help it move smoothly through the water.

pectoral fins

The hammerhead shark sways its powerful tail fin from side to side to move forward. The **pectoral fins** help it steer. Two **dorsal fins**, one large and one small, provide balance. The shark's large oil-filled liver makes it **buoyant**. Without its liver, the shark would sink toward the ocean floor.

HAMMERHEAD SHARK
TRACKED

Hammerheads are **viviparous**. Eggs hatch in the mother's body, and the shark pups grow inside of her. After 10 to 12 months, the mother gives birth to anywhere from a few pups to more than 50. The size of the litter depends on the size of the mother. Larger species tend to have larger litters.

The newborn pups of the great hammerhead shark measure up to 28 inches (70 centimeters) in length. Scalloped bonnethead pups are around 9 inches (23 centimeters) long. Pups spend the first months of their lives in shallow coastal waters, where they are safe from predators. Experts believe some species, such as the great hammerhead, can live 25 years or more.

Hammerhead pups have a rounder head shape than adults. Their heads flatten as they grow.

Hammerheads swing their broad heads from side to side as they swim. This way, they can use many of their senses to locate prey. The wide-set eyes give hammerheads a better view of their surroundings. The sharks can easily follow a scent trail with their wide-spaced nostrils. Their heads are also loaded with **ampullae of Lorenzini**. These tiny pores around the snout sense the **electric fields** of nearby animals.

Hammerheads are aggressive **apex predators**. Their mouths are small compared to other sharks, but they have plenty of sharp teeth. The long, **serrated** teeth in the front of the mouth are well suited for tearing flesh. The flatter teeth toward the back are used to grind shellfish and other hard prey. The hammerhead's favorite food is the stingray. It also eats bony fish, octopuses, squids, crabs, and small sharks. Hammerheads have even been known to eat their own young.

Hammerheads are shy and usually avoid people. Most are not considered dangerous unless they are provoked. Swimmers and divers should be especially cautious around the great hammerhead, smooth hammerhead, and scalloped hammerhead. These are the largest, most aggressive hammerhead sharks. Together, they are responsible for around 40 attacks on people.

HAMMERHEAD SHARK

CURRENT STATUS

Humans pose the greatest threat to hammerhead sharks. Sport fishers enjoy the challenge of pulling these powerful fish from the ocean. The sharks are also caught in nets and on lines meant for other fish. Most harmful to hammerheads is a practice called **finning**. Millions are killed each year during this process. Their large dorsal fins are in high demand in some Asian countries. People buy them to make shark fin soup. Hammerheads are also fished for their skin, meat, and livers.

The hammerhead shark population continues to get smaller every year because of overfishing. As a result, two species have been listed as **endangered** by the International Union for Conservation of Nature (IUCN). They are the great hammerhead and the scalloped hammerhead. These sharks are at risk of becoming extinct unless people change their practices.

SHARK BRIEF

Common Name: Hammerhead Shark

Also Known As: See nine species

Claim to Fame: Wide, flat head

Hot Spots: Costa Rica
Galápagos Islands
Malaysia

Life Span: Up to 30 years

Current Status: Least Concern to
Endangered (IUCN)

EXTINCT

EXTINCT IN
THE WILD

CRITICALLY
ENDANGERED

ENDANGERED

VULNERABLE

NEAR
THREATENED

LEAST
CONCERN

Hammerhead sharks help keep the ocean **ecosystem** healthy. They prevent prey populations from becoming too large. They also eat sick and weak animals. Right now the future of the hammerhead shark is uncertain.

Many countries are taking important steps to protect this unique fish. The United States, Australia, and other nations have banned finning. The government of Costa Rica is also taking a leadership role. It passed new laws in 2012 to protect hammerheads. As other countries follow their lead, hammerheads have a greater chance at surviving long into the future.

GLOSSARY

ampullae of Lorenzini—a network of tiny jelly-filled sacs around a shark's snout; the jelly is sensitive to the electric fields of nearby prey.

apex predators—predators that are not hunted by any other animal

buoyant—able to float

cartilage—flexible connective tissue that makes up a shark's skeleton

cephalofoils—the wide, flat heads of hammerhead sharks

countershading—coloring that helps camouflage an animal; fish with countershading have pale bellies and dark backs.

dermal denticles—small tooth-like scales that cover some types of fish

dorsal fins—the fins on the back of a fish

ecosystem—a community of organisms and their environment

electric fields—waves of electricity created by movement; every living being has an electric field.

endangered—at risk of becoming extinct

estuaries—places where a river meets the ocean

finning—the practice of cutting off a shark's fins at sea and tossing the shark back into the water

lagoons—shallow bodies of water separated from the sea by sand or reefs

migrate—to travel from one place to another, often with the seasons

pectoral fins—a pair of fins that extend from each side of a fish's body

serrated—having a jagged edge

species—groups of related animals; all animals in a species have the same characteristics.

viviparous—producing young that develop inside the body; viviparous animals give birth to live young.

TO LEARN MORE

At the Library

Mallory, Kenneth. *Swimming with Hammerhead Sharks*. Boston, Mass.: Houghton Mifflin, 2001.

Mathea, Heidi. *Hammerhead Sharks*. Edina, Minn.: ABDO Publishing, 2011.

Musgrave, Ruth. *National Geographic Kids Everything Sharks*. Washington, D.C.: National Geographic, 2011.

On the Web

Learning more about hammerhead sharks is as easy as 1, 2, 3.

1. Go to www.factsurfer.com.

2. Enter "hammerhead sharks" into the search box.

3. Click the "Surf" button and you will see a list of related Web sites.

With factsurfer.com, finding more information is just a click away.

INDEX

The images in this book are reproduced through the courtesy of: Imagebroker.net/ SuperStock, front cover, p. 21; Minden Pictures/SuperStock, pp. 4-5, 14-15; NaturePL/ SuperStock, pp. 6-7; Norbert Wu/Science Faction/SuperStock, pp. 8-9; Steve Bloom Images/Science Faction/SuperStock, pp. 10-11; Biosphoto/Jeffrey Rotman, pp. 12-13; Doug Perrine/SeaPics.com, pp. 16, 19; Jeremy Stattford-Deitsch/SeaPics.com, p. 17.